RAILWAY CONNECT

STEAM DAYS ON THE LEICESTER TO BURTON LINE

A timeless scene at Coalville as passengers move forward with the arrival of their Leicester-bound train hauled by Class 2P No. 40407 one Saturday morning in the summer of 1953.

Photograph: Ken Hunt

Sincere thanks must go to Derby Industrial Museum whose Mark Higginson kindly supplied the Midland Railway timetables; to Horace Gamble, Ron Hemsley, Kevin Lane, Mike Mitchell, Barry Hilton, R. M. Casserley (who also provided examples of his late father's work, H. C. Casserley) and Ken Hunt for their ready and cheerful assistance in lending photographs - and to the many who stopped along the way for a chat whenever steam railways were mentioned.

Thanks for support, in so many ways, which helped to make the idea of this book a reality are also extended to:

Shepshed Building Society who helped get this project on the rails.

Those who subscribed to the book in advance of publication (listed at end of book).

Robert Curtis of Echo Press, Loughborough for his encouragement.

ISBN 1 872479 17 0

Coalville Publishing Co Ltd.
The Springboard Centre
Mantle Lane
Coalville
Leicestershire
LE67 3DW

Tel: 01530 839531

Printed by: Echo Press, Loughborough, Great Britain.

Front cover: Almost 40 years it may have been since the Midland lost its identity in the grouping of railway companies, but in 1960 its locomotives still made up the greater part of the 17C (Coalville) allocation. But there were occasions when more glamourous visitors made a surprise visit - such as Jubilee Class No. 45615 *Malay States* which provided a little spice to the local scene on April 23. Photograph: Ron Hemsley

Back cover: Ivanhoe Line Special 1994. Photograph: AM Photographics

INTRODUCTION

The line between Leicester and Burton-on-Trent was opened officially on 1 August 1849, one of the first developments of the still-new Midland Railway Company which itself had been formed by amalgamation with three other companies only five years before.

Connection to an ever-growing railway network opened up new markets countrywide for North West Leicestershire's rich deposits of coal which together with locally quarried granite, clay products (pipes, bricks, tiles and earthenware) plus well-used passenger services, meant the line was always a busy one.

The railway brought about great changes in the district, encouraging an increasing population to meet the needs of expanding industry. The area, indeed, owed much to its steam operated railway which, in at least one instance, can claim to have named a town. Coalville had its railway before its name!

In the 1820s only a few isolated cottages were to be found along a rough track or Long Lane which left the Ashby turnpike at Bardon to rejoin it near Ravenstone. Advances in mining techniques meant deeper pits could be sunk but first, improved transport facilities were needed. So it was that through the efforts of Whitwick coal-owner William Stenson and others that the Leicester and Swannington Railway was built.

From its West Bridge terminus in Leicester this early railway provided stations at Glenfield, Ratby, Desford, Merrylees and Bagworth which was reached in 1832. The mixed coal and passenger trains were then extended to Ashby Road (later Bardon Hill) and then Long Lane in April 1833. Platforms were not provided in those days and, unlike others on the line, these two later places used nearby inns for station business. That at Bardon, on the former turnpike route, was on the opposite side of the road to the station and said to have been a one-time coaching inn.

At Long Lane the Railway Hotel served the same purpose. According to local businessman and historian Edgar Hawthorn, writing in the 1950s, a room to the left of the front entrance was used for the issue of tickets while a bell fixed behind the front door gave warning of an approaching train to intending passengers.

That arrangement lasted until 1848 when, the L & S Railway having been sold to the Midland, a new station was built - and named Coalville. It was a choice no doubt prompted by the title carved in the stone on the front of William Stenson's home: Coalville House. This stood on land next to today's local authority offices a few hundred yards from the railway, succumbing to demolition in the 1950s.

Further building by the Midland Railway saw the original West Bridge line by-passed from Desford. A station was provided at Kirby Muxloe before the new line curved to link up with what was to become the London, St. Pancras route and so into Leicester Midland station. Passengers continued to be carried over the West Bridge branch until 1928 but general goods and coal traffic lasted to 1966 when the line was closed after more than 130 years in service.

Other stations opened towards Burton were Swannington (avoiding the incline), Ashby-de-la-Zouch, Moira (where the jointly-owned M.R./L.N.W.R. line from Nuneaton via Shackerstone came in), and Gresley with the line officially declared open throughout in 1849.

Some years later a loop line connected Swadlincote and Woodville to the main route and in 1883 an L.N.W.R. venture brought the Charnwood Forest Railway from Loughborough and Shepshed to Coalville East (a site just a drop-kick from the Town Rugby ground) and on to Shackerstone and Nuneaton. Access to the Leicester to Burton line was made a mile outside the town.

These few words make no pretensions to being an history of the Leicester to Burton line. Rather are they, with the photographs which follow, a brief reminder of how it used to be - at a time when passenger services could return to The Ivanhoe Line, restoring to the district all the right connections.

A VIEW FROM THE LINESIDE

The last years of steam on the Burton - Leicester Railway and its branches remembered.

Last man in and ten runs still needed. The fate of the game hung in the balance, the atmosphere as tense as any test match on the hallowed turf of Lords or Trent Bridge - even though this was on The Scotlands, a patch of wasteland alongside the railway in Coalville with barely enough flat space to accommodate a cricket pitch.Nervously the batsman scraped his mark on the crease. The bowler rushed in, his arm a blur... and from out on the boundary went up then frantic shout: Namer!

What happened to the ball no-one could remember. The fielding side were left gasping in amazement as the batsman and the rest of the Bakewell Street team abandoned the wicket and fled across to the fence. There at the home signal of No. 1 Box stood the wondrous sight of No. 5503 *Leicestershire Regiment*, its large boiler, smoke deflectors and 4-6-0 wheels breathing majesty and power, the first main line locomotive we had seen on a local track.

Leicestershire Regiment, the locomotive which caused a cricket match to be abandoned when it appeared in Coalville, was a member of the Patriot 4-6-0 Class introduced in 1930 by the LMS, like sister engine No. 45507 *Royal Tank Corps* seen some years afterwards on July 5, 1953, while on shed at Derby for minor repairs.

Photograph: Ken Hunt

For something like 20 minutes everyone stood and stared at this magical machine before, released by the signal, it effortlessly glided away. By then the other team had claimed the game and gone home - but who cared about cricket just then? We'd seen a Patriot!The euphoria of seeing the Patriot, a type usually to be seen only by visiting Rugby or Nuneaton, emphasises why Coalville was regarded as something of a railway backwater.

Coalville was in the Derby Motive Power District and had its own shed - which is how depots were known - with its code of 17C carried on 30 or so engines at that time. Except for a few of Stainer's Class 8F 2-8-0s built for the London Midland and Scottish Railway (LMS), most were of former Midland Railway origin: freight 2F, 3F and 4F locomotives. The Midland, it should be explained, had lost its identity in the grouping of 1922 when, along with the London North Western and other companies, it became part of the new LMS. Was it any wonder, then, that the sight of something more glamorous caused such excitement?

From 1832 when the first L&SR first reached Long Lane (a station later renamed Coalville and from which, it can be argued, the district took its name) railways and coal together prompted rapid growth and between them were the area's lifeblood. By 1849 the Midland had absorbed the L&SR and extended the branch to connect Leicester and Burton. Locomotive servicing facilities were provided in Coalville in the 1860s with a three-road shed and other improvements completed by the early 1890s; all of which survived in use until 1965.

All this and its attendant activity was immediately behind the station where, within feet of the platform ends, were the notorious level crossing gates through which the A50 trunk road passed. Chaos ensued whenever they closed across the road which they did with surprising regularity.

The best place to view all the havoc, and the trains, was the lattice footbridge which not only served both platforms at the station, gave access to the high signal box and served as a pedestrian crossing but also provided a good vantage point from which to see engine movements. In later years I came to know the signalmen and invitations to join them in its cosy warmth were extended but not before a chilly apprenticeship had been served.

Passenger turns between Leicester and Burton were the province of ex-Midland Class 2P 4-4-0s, and engines such as 395, 404, 407, 500 and 633 with its odd-looking experimental feed-water heater cluttering up one side of its smokebox became old friends. Friends! You wouldn't have thought so by our rude remarks when a particular engine appeared for the fourth time in a day. But how good it would be to see one in action today and hear again the ring of those tall wheels. What a pity none have made it into preservation.

Half a mile out of Coalville station in the Burton direction were the marshalling sidings of Mantle Lane. Through these lay the original L&SR route to Swannington incline and as late as 1947 a Class 4F loco was seen gingerly inching its way over the badly worn rails of the Spring Lane crossing near the engine house with what were probably the last coal wagons to travel that way before closure. The cable and its mid-track rollers were in place for a time but it meant a trip to York Museum years later to finally see the winding engine in preservation.

Coalville junction, a couple of miles in the opposite direction, was the point where a single track line built by the Midland and London and North Western companies diverged and ran down to Shackerstone - at which point steam is still active today on The Battlefield Line. A second single-track came in here, the Ashby and Nuneaton Joint Railway which connected with the Burton line at Moira West Junction. Double track continued southwards from Shackerstone to Nuneaton.

In charge of the box, Mr Harry Lovell. Like Jack Bird, his counterpart in Coalville station box, and indeed signalmen everywhere, Harry was always ready for a chat and an excuse to put the kettle on - but always with an eye on his block instruments.

Photograph: Ken Hunt

These lines were the legacy of intense competition between rival companies throughout the 19th century; in this case the LNWR wanted to claim a share of the revenue an increasingly prosperous coalfield was generating. Among the many plans for lines submitted to Parliament by the railway companies was one by the LNWR to put a line in from Nuneaton to Loughborough, there connecting to the Great Central. For various reasons that ambition was never realised, instead a terminus station was provided at Derby Road in Loughborough where Connections to Euston were proudly advertised on a single line passing through Shepshed, Whitwick and Coalville East, thence passing under the Leicester line and on to Hugglescote, near where the chord line from Coalville Junction joined. It was from Nuneaton that the memorable Patriot had come and once it was realised that other types of loco used the branch a special eye was kept on it.

Back on the Midland (or, rather, LMS), one passenger train worth an early Saturday morning visit was the 8.50 to Leicester. Usually a Nottingham (16A) turn, it often produced a compound 4-4-0, handsome former express engines otherwise rarely seen on this line. First of Class N. 1000 was a regular, though not in the gleaming red livery of the Midland Railway it wears today as a resident of York Museum.

The highlight of summer Saturday traffic at Coalville was the return train from Blackpool Central. Made up of ten or more carriages, its length meant the train having to be drawn up twice to allow the considerable number of returning holiday-makers to alight safely on the much shorter platform. That manoeuvre involved carriages standing cross the road and crossing gates stayed closed for an age. The Saturday tea-time traffic snarl-up which resulted had to be seen to be believed!

The crossing gates in Coalville close again and road users are in for a longer wait than usual as the Summer Saturdays only service from Blackpool Central brings home returning holidaymakers in July 1960. So long was the train that it had to draw forward across the road to allow everyone to alight safely on the platform. The locomotive is a powerful Class 9 2-10-0 No. 92104, a BR Standard engine primarily built for heavy freight but which also proved useful on passenger traffic.

Photograph: Ken Hunt

These Blackpool trains always produced some exciting motive power and were double-headed to and from Derby, the extra engine necessary to help negotiate the tortuous curves of the Swadlincote loop. One full platform of holiday-makers awaiting the 6 am departure had a treat when in came a train drawn by a very new Stephenson Black 5, resplendent in shining paintwork and polished steel.

The return working could also throw up anything from a Crab or a Black 5 or even a Fowler 2-6-4 tank engine. Belle Vue (Manchester) seemed to be the main provider of the 4-6-0s but, wonder of wonders, 68A (Carlisle Kingmoor) engines were noted too. These engines always spent the weekend on Coalville shed before being put on some working which would set them on the return to home base.

In the last couple of years before passenger services were ended the monster 2-10-0 Class 9s occasionally appeared on this working. Motive Power District changes by then(1963), however, had seen Coalville moving into the Leicester Division and its shed code changing to 15D. After that the Blackpool engines went on to Leicester for servicing. Strangely enough, ideal though they were for the heavy coal trains, the holiday train was their only appearance on the branch.. It was in August 1962 that I saw my last Blackpool and that by chance, sitting on a motorbike in Hotel Street in a queue of vehicles waiting for the gates to open. The train pulled across the road - with a Royal Scot at its head! No. 46165 *The Ranger (12th London Regiment).* No longer wanted on the Irish Mail or other prestigious trains, No. 46165 was in a sadly uncared-for-state - but all the same a remarkable engine to grace the local scene.

Coalville's principle freight trains of the day were The Wellingborough, The Beer and The West Bridge. At least that's how they were known by us. The first of these was an evening train with up to 50 coal wagons behind a Class 8F 2-8-0.

The engine was usually known to us but it was the spectacle we'd gathered to watch! First the signal man would heave on the iron wheel in the box and the gates slowly closed across the road, seemingly ages before the engine began to stir out of the Mantle Lane siding down the line. Road traffic in the 1940s and 1950s may have been sparse compared with that of today, but even so the queues of vehicles stretched to the Clock Tower on one side and up past Chapel Corner, or even the council offices, on the other.

The line from Mantle Lane was on an incline up through the station and the Class 8 had to work hard to drag its massive load up the slope. Towering columns of smoke would erupt from the chimney as she blasted her way through the station, the whole place shaking as buildings were engulfed in clouds of steam - pursued by clanking, jostling wagons steadily gaining momentum with the assistance of a Jinty (a shunting engine) chattering busily away at the rear. What a sight it was: sheer awesome power and a scene still remembered today.

An express among all the slow-moving coal trains was The Beer, a train conveying the beverage of Burton-on-Trent to London, passing through Coalville around 8pm. More often than not there would be a Burton Crab at the front and as all signals were pulled off an expectant hush fell as first sight of the engine rocking round the approach curve was awaited. With a satisfying roar the 2-6-0 would storm through the station, leaving in its wake an equally satisfying aroma of engine smoke and hops.

Slowest train of the day was The West Bridge. The old 2F would leave Coalville shed around 5 o'clock in the morning to trundle its way on to the Glenfield branch, and wandered back home about seven in the evening.

Ancient they may have been, but these engines worked hard and long, the crew on the early shift travelling back by bus!

Before the Midland's connection to their London Road station was made the Swannington Railway ran through Ratby and Glenfield to a terminus at West Bridge which lay in the shadow of Leicester's Great Central station (which came later, of course). This single-track branch, though losing passenger services back in 1928, still served as an important carrier of coal and other goods to the city. But there was one major snag about it: Glenfield Tunnel.

Such were the dimensions of this tunnel that only certain engines could squeeze through and it was this which accounted for the retention of the Midland Class 2s at Coalville after others of a similar vintage disappeared elsewhere. In latter years when an ailing 2F could no longer be patched up at Derby, another of the same type was dug up from some far corner of the country (and some of them *looked* as though they had been dug up!) and transferred to Coalville. No. 58182, which became the last to work, had come from Barrow-in-Furness. She was cut up in September 1964, a sad end for a sturdy old locomotive.

Then one day one of the BR Standard 2MT 2-6-0s, No. 78028, appeared on Coalville shed. These engines were, of course, out of gauge for Glenfield Tunnel but someone had hit on the bright idea of reducing the cab height and boiler fittings - and that brought the end in sight for the old 0-6-0s. Though local drivers had a rough affection for their old steeds they soon took to the new one and after years of huddling under a tarpaulin slung from the half-cabs of the 2Fs the newcomer was regarded as something of a Rolls Royce. When a second modified 2-6-0 appeared, the faithful 2Fs finally retired to the back siding. After 60 and more years, they had earned their keep.

Big improvement they may have been, but the new engines had worked from Coalville for only nine months before the shed closed. The locos then worked from Leicester until the Glenfield line itself was abandoned 18 months later.

There was no need to be asked twice when a friendly driver offered a footplate trip next time he was on the West Bridge. Aboard the BSA C15 motorbike bought just days before, it was an exhilarating feeling motoring along the A50 in the early morning sunshine; the only vehicle on the road. Still only 5.30 a.m. when I parked the bike on the platform (never a doubt for it's safety, then), it wasn't long before the train was heard coming along the branch. "We're not stopping today," shouted driver, Jack Baugh. "Get on!" But 59298 was doing no more than five miles per hour and I was soon aboard, with a helping hand from fireman George Barkby.

There was hardly time to get my bearings before, with a shriek of the whistle, blackness descended as the loco rumbled into the tunnel mouth. The red glare from the firebox reflected back from brick walls only inches away from cab sides, and a deafening roar came from that tall chimney as the engine rocked through the mile-long tube. Due at work for 8 a.m. myself, I had time only for a "thank you" to the crew before setting off for the nearest bus to Glenfield. The invitation to "come again" was never taken up but it was certainly a trip to remember.

Today it is difficult to imagine a railway ever existed in that area, for Glenfield station and the line into Leicester (parallel with part of Groby Road) is all covered in houses. The tunnel itself, its days of usefulness at an end, is securely barred at both ends.

Nuneaton (2B) had belonged to the Midland's great rival, the London North Western, and its locomotive stock still

West Bridge, Leicester at 7. am on a July day in 1959 and the crew of Coalville's 58298 has just arrived with the first mixed train of the day. Before getting down to a morning's shunting, though, there was time for George Barkby (top left), driver Jack Baugh alongside him, guard William Hill (bottom left) and the Leicester-based shunter to pose for the phtographer, who had just experienced a footplate ride through Glenfield tunnel.

Photograph: Ken Hunt

reflected that fact - most of them examples of the LNW style. Being on the West Coast Main Line, No. 5503 was not the only named engine to appear on the line from Shackerstone, probably sent out to fill time between more important work: 5539 *Giggleswick* and 5538 *E. C. Trench* were a couple, with Jubilee 4-6-0s and Black 5s adding to the interest. But the type seen most regularly was the ex-LNW G2 Class 7, such as 9120 and 9395 (still being restored by preservationists). Not only did they look different, they sounded different, too. Even before seeing them the 0-8-0s were easily identified by their distinctive exhaust beat.

One little train we liked to see was the daily Milk which ran round the circuit of the lines from Nuneaton, up to Shackerstone and Coalville, then on to Moira and Overseal, Shackerstone and home. Known as The Milk from the lampcode it always carried, this one-carriage train was something of a reminder of what had once been on the branches. Never overburdened, parcels, mail and small consignments were its cargo - in addition to supplying cans of water to outlying signal boxes.

The LNW Webb 2-4-2 tank engines used on this working were a delight to see and, like other ex-North West locos, had a character all their own. The small engines with water carried in side tanks, such as 6749, 6687 and 6658, were of a type one might expect to see in a Will Hay film of old. Tough little things built in the 1890s, they went from the local scene by 1948 but the service continued well into BR days with such strangers as LMS 2-6-2T No. 5 and No. 17, Stanier's 40201 and 40206, before Ivatt's brand new Class 4 2-6-0 engines arrived. Built in modern, easy maintenance design these locos broke away from age-old styles as the LMS sought to modernise its steam stock.

Schooldays came to end and my working career began at the *Coalville Times*, then sited in Margaret Street. Every Friday large parcels of weekly newspapers had to be taken to buses for distribution to local villages - and some to the railway station. As the youngest apprentice, that was one of my tasks, and it was often necessary to think up some good reason for a belated return! Dumping the heavy parcels in the station office one day a wisp of steam down-line intrigued. It meant a short wait, more puzzled by the minute. What passed eventually was No. 22822, a Kirtley-designed 0-6-0 of 1863 vintage and forerunner of the 2Fs usually seen. Its outside frames, curved to accommodate eccentrically connected coupling rods whirling round in frantic fashion, brought to mind grandmother's cast iron washday mangle gone berserk!

More excuses for lateness were needed a few weeks later when a large boiler looming over the everyday Midland engines on shed had to be investigated. The stranger was an LMS 7F 0-8-0 No. 9586 bearing a 15A (Wellingborough) shedplate. Very unusual to find an example of this 1930s type developed from a North Western design in the area. It seemed two had been allocated to Wellingborough for trials on coal trains. It could not have been successful for although the second loco, No. 9599, visited Coalville shortly afterwards, they were never seen again.

Like many another caught up by the fascination of railways, attempts to explain it were abandoned long ago. That small group of friends had grown up through the war years when everything was simply unobtainable or at best in very short supply. Travel was still difficult and rarely did we venture far from our home town. But our spare time was filled - with cricket and football, cycling and board games galore in each other's homes in wintertime, and unforgettable feasts put on by respective mothers (oh! those home-made doughnuts and chelsea buns!). They were happy and secure days despite wartime conditions and the years of austerity that followed. Mountains of parcels at the station were labelled to far away places: Cascelloids dolls and toys, Pegson portable pumps destined for Inverness and Portsmouth, Manchester or Leeds. Baskets full of pigeons setting off for Berwick, brought in by the dozen by local men; engines steaming out or arriving from towns we had only heard of - it all added up to the magic of steam and was an incentive to explore and discover for ourselves.

By 1948 the group of friends had discovered distant, worldly Tamworth. The 18 long miles to that glorious mecca of the steam fan was managed by pedal power - cycles which mostly had seen their best days a long time previously. Tamworth was a crossroads of the West Coast main line and a one-time Midland line from Derby to Birmingham and the Bristol area. Boys flocked there in their hundreds. It was there we saw the LNW *Queen of the Belgians* of the handsome Prince of Wales, the Princess Royals, the Streaks (streamlined Coronation class) and Royal Scots, all thundering past in ear-shattering splendour.

Football specials began again after the war but, Coalville being in the Derby district as far as railways were concerned, they were all to Derby County games. We thought these trains were great. Not for any interest in football but because the away games gave opportunity of having a look at other towns and their railways - and all for the price of a cheap day return. One such remembered trip took us to Stoke-on-Trent where a local train was quickly boarded to Crewe; what a great steam centre that was!

School days ended and a budding career brought even more hours of study after the day's work was done. There was no longer time for watching the trains go by, but it did not matter, steam was giving way to diesel and the old fascination was no longer there. For a while longer the camera came out on occasions until one evening in the early 1960s a sentimental journey was made to Coalville station just to see if The Beer still ran. It did indeed, but headed by a sleek new diesel locomotive, no doubt a big improvement on the steam engines it replaced, but devoid of all feeling and atmosphere - and my faithful old Kodak folding camera recorded its last railway subject.

Returning to my old home town some years later, it was difficult to imagine the scene as it had been. Pit heads were silent, if indeed still to be seen at all; the railway barely a shadow of what it used to be. The once-notorious level-crossing now guarded by modern lifting barriers which maybe stirred from time to time; the bustling station and busy local loco shed, the high signal box and footbridge all swept away - the days of steam only a pleasant memory.

Ken Hunt

Going up for the Cup! The hopes of Leicester City supporters were high as they headed for Wembley and the F.A. Cup Final on 25th May, 1963 aboard a special train which ran on the Burton to Leicester branch which is double-headed by 2-6-0 No. 43118 and Black Five 4-6-0 44891 as it crosses over the Great Central Main Line. Sadly for the supporters of The Foxes they came home disappointed by the result: Manchester United 3, Leicester City 1.

Photograph: Horace Gamble

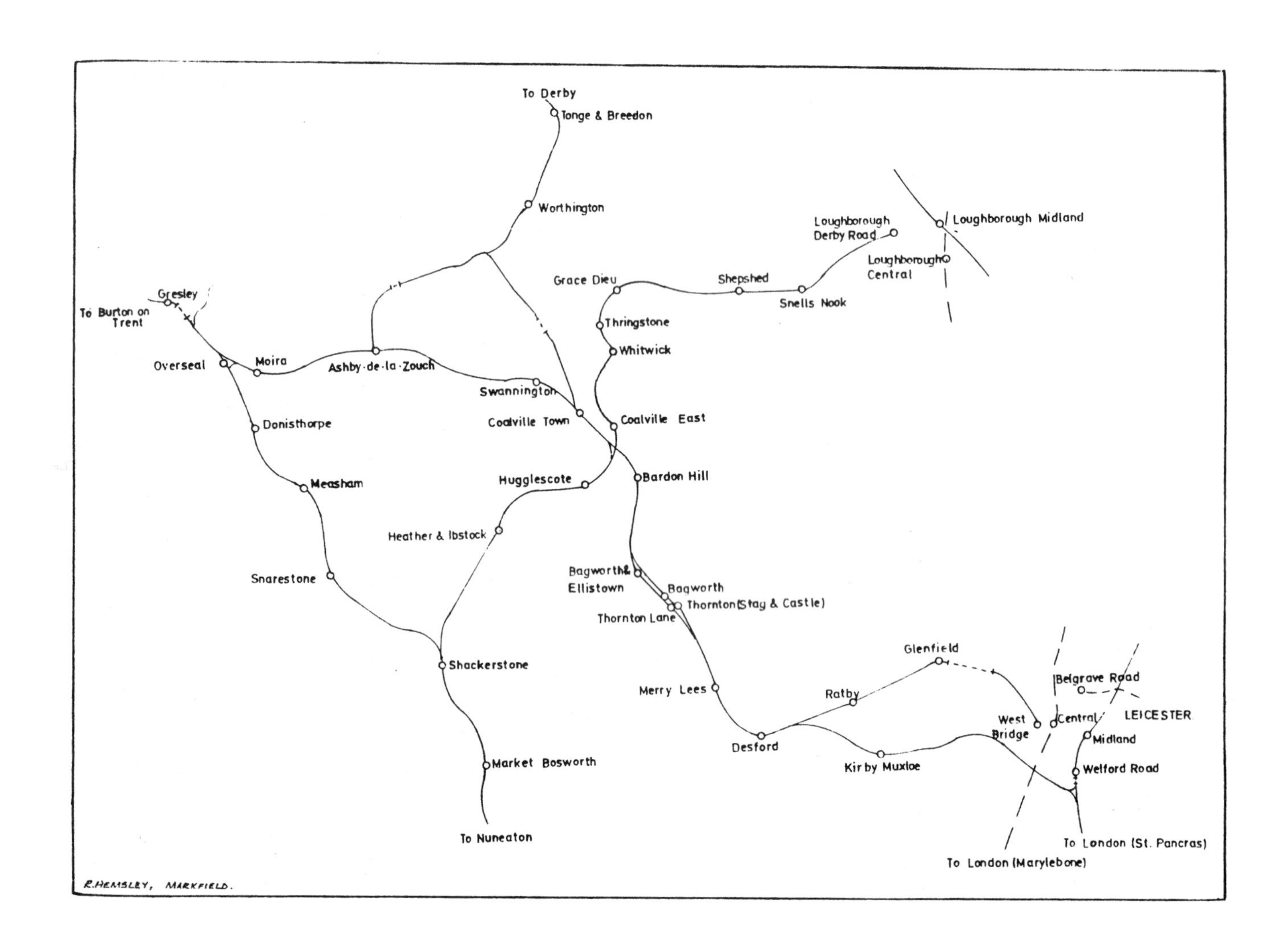
To Derby
Tonge & Breedon
Worthington
Loughborough Midland
Loughborough
Derby Road
Loughborough
Central
Grace Dieu
Shepshed
Snells Nook
Gresley
To Burton on
Trent
Thringstone
Whitwick
Overseal
Moira
Ashby-de-la-Zouch
Swannington
Coalville Town
Coalville East
Donisthorpe
Measham
Hugglescote
Bardon Hill
Heather & Ibstock
Snarestone
Bagworth &
Ellistown
Bagworth
Thornton (Stag & Castle)
Thornton Lane
Glenfield
Shackerstone
Belgrave Road
Merry Lees
Ratby
LEICESTER
West
Bridge
Central
Midland
Desford
Kirby Muxloe
Welford Road
Market Bosworth
To Nuneaton
To London (St. Pancras)
To London (Marylebone)
R. HEMSLEY, MARKFIELD.

Work on Coalville's crossing is interrupted as picks and shovels (not a JCB in sight!) are laid aside while Ivatt 2-6-0 No. 43041 takes a Sunday morning train into the station, hand-flagged through the danger signal which is out of action. An innovation in engine design, the first three of the class were built at Derby in December 1947 by the LMS. Watters' flour mill in the background was demolished some years later to enable a covered market to be erected.

Photograph: Ken Hunt

Maid of all work. A Fowler design 0-6-0 4F No. 43854 arrives at Coalville Junction to collect her train of coal from the South Leicestershire coalfield.

Photograph: Ron Hemsley

Ex-LMS 44403 was travelling light engine in August 1963 at Saffron Lane Junction as Black 5 4-6-0 No. 44663 accelerated past with a Leicester to Alton Towers excursion calling at Coalville and Ashby.

Photograph: Horace Gamble

A Hughes design Class 5F 2-6-0 rumbles on to the River Soar viaduct as it enters Leicester with an evening freight train from the Burton direction on 24th May, 1960.

Photograph: Mike Mitchell

On the outskirts of Leicester, Kirby Muxloe station was probably the most attractive on the branch, set as it was in a rural area. A view in the up direction when gas lamps are still in situ just before closure.

Photograph: Barry Hilton

One of Ivatt's 2-6-0s for branchline work for the LMS was No. 46454 at Knighton North Junction on 12th June, 1959, showing the neglect which increasingly affected steam stock.

Photograph: Horace Gamble

Early morning snow lingers in the shadows of Coalville Town station on a bright but chilly day in February 1955 as locally based Class 4F No. 44260 blasts up from Mantle Lane with a lengthy mixed freight behind her.

Photograph: Ken Hunt

A 1929 development of the London North Western G2 0-8-0, No. 49509 was awaiting scrapping in the early 1950s at Gorton works, Manchester. Two of the once 140 strong class appeared briefly in Coalville when transferred to Wellingborough for trials on heavy coal trains in 1947.

Photograph: Ken Hunt

Desford station not long before closure. In the Leicester direction the signal box stands on the opposite side of the road and the hand-operated crossing gates while examples of Midland-style parcels barrows stand near the up platform waiting shelter. Across in front of the station master's house and offices can be seen a section of the lower, original, L&S platform which contrasts with the later extension.

Photograph: Barry Hilton

The Coalville-based crew of Stanier Class 8F 2-8-0 No. 48607 pause a moment for photographer Horace Gamble on Saturday, 6th February, 1965, at Knighton South Junction. Driver Harry Johnson is on the left with Guard Wilf Vesty centre and Passed Fireman Ellis Hill right.

Photograph: Horace Gamble

His freight train brought to a stand at Desford Junction, Coalville driver Harry Johnson climbs from the cab of his Class 8 to check with the signalman. Track to the left of the box is the original Leicester and Swannington route to Leicester while the far left line was a storage siding.

Photograph: Horace Gamble

With a heavy coal train destined for southern counties on the drawbar, Ellis Hill eases steam off his Class 8 as it passes through Knighton Junction and on to the St. Pancras line.

Photograph: Horace Gamble

Saffron Lane Junction and No. 75041, a British Rail Standard 4MT 4-6-0, designed at Brighton, picks up speed with the 5.30 pm from Leicester for all stations to Burton.

Photograph: Horace Gamble

Built in the late 1920s for the Somerset and Dorset Railway, No.40633 was a Burton (17B) engine in the 1950s and a familiar sight on local passenger work in the area. Pictured at Desford station with a Leicester train.

Photograph: Ken Hunt

From the earliest days of railway signalling was this Midland Railway crossbar signal at Bardon Hill guarding entry and exit to extensive quarry sidings. Instead of a semaphore arm, moving up or down, to indicate a clear road as those in the background, this pivoted horizontally. Presenting its full width red-painted face meant stop. Listed as of historical interest, the old signal disappeared around the time the line was singled. Bardon station, beyond the Grange Road crossing, closed in 1952 but the signal box, one of the oldest Midland boxes remaining, is still in regular use.

Photograph: Barry Hinton

Ex-LNWR 0-8-0 7F No. 49385 stands on the site of the old North Western depot at Coalville Junction where the line from Shackerstone and Nuneaton joined the Midland line. The water tower was still in use on 10th August, 1950, but the turntable and small loco shed which stood to the rear of the loco had long since disappeared.

Photograph: Ron Hemsley

Coalville-based Class 4F 0-6-0 No. 43865 hurries its short train of empty coal and stone wagons along at Ellistown in 1956........

Photograph: Mike Mitchell

..........and passes the entrance to Ellistown Colliery sidings, with its attendant signal box, on its journey towards Coalville.

Photograph: Mike Mitchell

Coal for the Capital was a major part of the regular traffic out of Coalville hauled by powerful Stanier 8F 2-8-0s with 1,000 tons or more behind them, locomotives such as No. 48219 blasting up the long drag to Bardon station. Just short months later, in October 1965, 48219 was among 14 Class 8s transferred away when Coalville shed closed.

Photograph: Ron Hemsley

Tall wheels and larger boilers lent a stately air to these former Midland Class 3P 4-4-0s. Rebuilt in 1910, Nos. 705 and 707 made occasional appearances on Leicester to Burton duties and were the last survivors of their class in 1952. Nos. 707 and 708 are on Leicester shed in this 1935 photo.

Photograph: H.C. Casserley

A scene from a different age as No. 44572 quietly skirts the edge of Whitwick Colliery's mountainous spoil heap in 1954. Empty wagons were supplied to the colliery sidings (left) to be drawn back via the track curving to bottom left of the photo. Filled wagons then went out on a line alongside Whitwick Road to sidings near Coalville Bridges. Forty years on and the scene has changed. Stand here today and your life would be in danger, for this is now part of Coalvile's bypass with its attendant constant roar of traffic. But at least past days are acknowledged by the new road's name: Stephenson Way.

Photograph: Ken Hunt

Bowen-Cooke 0-8-0 No. 49447 thrashes up the bank from Hugglescote to Charnwood Junction with coal from South Leicester colliery in January 1960. Class 7s were frequently seen on this line on workings from Nuneaton shed which retained its LNWR origins to the end of steam.

Photograph: Ron Hemsley

LEICESTER, COALVILLE, ASHBY, SWADLINCOTE, AND BURTON

WEEKDAYS.

Station					Saturdays only		
London (St. Pancras) dep.	..	2 25	..	4 25	9 50	10 25	12 25
LEICESTER dep.		7 2		9 10	12 15	12 30	2 45
Kirby Muxloe		7 14		9 22	12 27	12 43	2 59
Desford		7 21		9 28	12 35	12 49	3 5
Bagworth & Ellistown		7 33		9 40	12 45	1 0	3 16
Bardon Hill		7 40		9 46	12 52	1 6	3 22
Coalville	5 50	7 45	7 56	9 55	12 56	1 12	3 29
Swannington	5 54		8 1	10 1		1 16	3 33
Ashby	6 1	7 54	8 8	10 10		1 24	3 41
Moira	[illegible]	[illegible]	8 17	10 17		1 31	3 48
Woodville			8 30			1 45	
Swadlincote			8 36			1 52	
Gresley	6 15	8 5		10 24			3 54
BURTON arr.	6 24	8 16	8 48	10 33		2 5	4 3
Uttoxeter (N.S.) arr.	8 16		9 44	11 25		3 41	5 7
Derby	7 15	8 55	9 26	10 57		3 5	4 27

Station				B		Saturdays only	SUNDAYS.	
London (St. Pancras) dep.	2 25	3 30	4 25	6 25			..	6 15
LEICESTER dep.	4 33	6 20	6 37	8 25	9 12	11 12	9 30	8 40
Kirby Muxloe	4 50	6 33	6 49	8 37	9 26	11 26	9 42	8 52
Desford	4 57	6 40	6 55	C	9 35	11 34	9 48	8 59
Bagworth & Ellistown	5 9	6 51	7 8	C	9 47	11 46	9 59	9 12
Bardon Hill	5 15	6 57	7 14		9 54	11 52	10 5	9 19
Coalville	5 21	7 2	7 20	8 59	9 59	11 57	10 10	9 25
Swannington	5 26		7 25		10 4		10 15	9 29
Ashby	5 33	7 9	7 33	9 7	10 11		10 24	9 37
Moira	5 39		7 40	9 12	10 17		10 30	9 43
Woodville	..	..	..				..	..
Swadlincote								
Gresley	5 45		7 47	C	10 23		10 37	9 50
BURTON arr.	5 55		7 56	9 24	10 32	12 20	10 47	10 2
Uttoxeter (N.S.) arr.	8 [illegible]		10A 2					
Derby	6 50			9 49	11 1	3 3	1 26	10 25

WEEKDAYS.

Station				Saturdays only		Saturdays only		
Derby dep.	..	6 12	7 48	[illegible]	9 45	..	12 55	2 56
Uttoxeter (N.S.)			7 [illegible]	[illegible]	9 59		12 24	2 43
BURTON dep.		6 41	8 15	10 55	11 3		1 22	3 25
Gresley			8 25	11 5			1 34	3 36
Swadlincote		6 59			11 15			
Woodville		7 10			11 24			
Moira		7 25	8 32	[illegible]	11 38		1 40	3 43
Ashby		7 34	8 40	[illegible]	11 45		1 46	3 50
Swannington		[illegible]		[illegible]	11 57		1 56	[illegible]
Coalville	7 0	7 52	8 53	[illegible]	12 2	1 17	2 1	4 6
Bardon Hill	7 5	7 59	8 59	[illegible]	12 8	1 22	[illegible]	4 12
Bagworth & Ellistown	7 11	8 6	9 5	12 5	12 14	1 29	2 13	4 18
Desford	7 19	8 15	9 13	12 13	12 22	1 37	2 20	4 25
Kirby Muxloe	7 28	8 22	9 16	12 18	12 29	1 42	2 26	4 31
LEICESTER arr.	7 37	8 33	9 30	12 31	12 40	1 53	2 39	4 42
London (St. Pancras) arr.	9 57	11 0	11 35	[illegible]	3 25	4 20	5 45	6 35

Station				SUNDAYS.	
Derby dep.	4 45	5 7	8 25	6 35	5 17
Uttoxeter (N.S.)		3 5	7 55	..	..
BURTON dep.	5 12	5 45	8 52	7 15	5 42
Gresley		5 58	9 2	7 26	5 54
Swadlincote	5 25			..	..
Woodville	5 30				
Moira	[illegible]	6 4	9 10	7 33	6 3
Ashby	5 55	6 12	9 18	7 43	6 12
Swannington		[illegible]	[illegible]	7 54	6 24
Coalville		6 23	9 38	8 0	6 30
Bardon Hill		6 35	9 43	8 [illegible]	6 35
Bagworth & Ellistown		6 41	9 49	8 14	6 43
Desford		6 50	9 55	8 24	6 53
Kirby Muxloe		6 57	10 2	8 31	[illegible]
LEICESTER arr.		7 9	10 15	8 46	[illegible]
London (St. Pancras) arr.		9 15	4 20	11 53	[illegible]

In addition to the above a frequent service is given by the Midland Company's Light Railway between Burton and Ashby.

Passengers holding Season Tickets between Burton and Moira and intermediate Stations to Leicester, via Gresley, charged at the ordinary scale, are allowed to travel via Swadlincote for through purposes only, but are NOT allowed to break their journey at Swadlincote or Woodville.

A Saturdays only.

B Saturdays excepted.

C Stops to set down London Passengers.

LEICESTER (WEST BRIDGE STATION) AND DESFORD.

WEEKDAYS.		
LEICESTER (West Bridge) dep.	1 0	5 30
Glenfield	[illegible]	5 39
Ratby	1 14	5 45
DESFORD arr.	1 19	5 50

WEEKDAYS.		
DESFORD dep.	8 25	2 5
Ratby	8 32	2 15
Glenfield	8 39	2 21
LEICESTER (West Bridge) arr.	8 45	2 28

Midland Railway timetable from October 2nd. 1922 - until further notice!

Compound Class 4P 4-4-0s only ever appeared in Coalville on an early morning train to Leicester, an unbalanced working, generally bringing Nottingham locos along the line. So it was something of an occasion when one 1954 Saturday, No. 41192 brought a Burton train into the platform.

Photograph: Ken Hunt

A view from the bridge. The Midland Railway motif was rescued from its end gable position just before the whole station site was cleared in 1969 and happily installed at Shackerstone station. Coalville High Street is to the left while Marshall's Row, itself long gone, stands beyond the station. Gas lamps still lit the platforms and footbridge. Four of the bays in the platform canopy were of reinforced glass while the two furthest from the camera were of some solid material. Could this have been the result of bomb damage during the 1940s?

Phtograph: Barry Hilton

Designed by the LMS but built by British Rail between 1948 and 1952, the Ivatt class 4 2-6-0s were to be part of the former company's modernisation programme. In 1949 No. 43018 leads a Black 5 into Coalville station with a Saturdays only return train from Blackpool Central.

Photograph: Ken Hunt

Once known as Harry Johnson's engine, her regular driver when based at Coalville during the war years, No. 2336 still carried her LMS identity in the summer of 1948, the year of Nationalisation. Transferred to Burton (17B) some time before, 2336 brings a Leicester-bound train into Coalville.

Photograph: Ken Hunt

During the 1940s Coalville could count one passenger loco among its allocation: No. 79, a Stanier Class 3P 2-6-2T, of the same type as 40123 in the photograph. By 1947, however, operating changes saw No. 79 transferred to Kentish Town in London.

Photograph: Ron Hemsley

For weeks before public holidays stations would advertise forthcoming trips with an impressive display of colourful handbills in waiting rooms. Their popularity was reflected in the eight-coach trains provided; such as this day excursion to North Wales which pulls into Coalville station in 1956.

Photograph: Ken Hunt

Geraniums bloomed in Coalville No. 1 Box through summer days tended by signalmen in spare moments between shunting operations on the Snibston (left) and Whitwick collieries exchange sidings. On Saturdays the box was switched out and the signals were all off as Class 2P 4-4-0 No. 40453 takes the 1.55 pm from Coalville to Leicester.

Photograph: Ken Hunt

The rapid growth in coal and other industries which followed the coming of the railway to North West Leicestershire soon led the Midland to site a single-road shed and servicing facilities on land immediately behind the station. Improvements and additions were made in subsequent years until in the early 1890s a new and larger three-road building replaced the earlier one. Of standard Midland design, it was lit by gas to the end. In this 1964 photo, not long before the end of steam at the shed, the centre road is occupied by Standard 78028 while the others are all Stanier 2-8-0s. The building to the left housed the foreman's office, enginemen's mess and stores while over on the right stood the Ellis and Everard building with its road vehicle weighbridge alongside.

Photograph: Ken Hunt

Getting coal into engine tenders was a primitive affair at sheds like Coalville. No automatic coaling tower here, just men's strong arms and brute force. Locomotives in need of refuelling drew alongside the opposite, open side of the building seen above. Manual labour transferred coal from a wagon into a small, wheeled tub which in turn was manhandled across to the platform's edge where its load was tipped into the tender below - hard work, particularly if the tender was near empty. To get the coal up there in the first place had its moments of drama. The quiet approach in pushing loaded wagons aloft could result in the loco losing adhesion, sliding back amid clouds of steam but go too speedily and the far end buffer stop was bent.

Rebuilt with a new boiler around 1917, No. 58305 still retains the original half-cab it had on leaving Derby works in the 19th Century. Typical equipment for this type of engine was the rolled-up tarpaulin on the roof; the only weather protection the crew had. Much of this loco's long life was spent locally at Leicester (15C), Burton (17B) and then Coalville (by now 15D) replacing the scrapped 58298 in late 1960. Not for long, however. Seven months later 58305 made her last journey to Crewe in June 1961.

Photograph: Ken Hunt

Almost one of those spot the differences puzzles. Bardon Hill and the Scotlands bowls club pavilion and field provide the background as LMS 4F No. 44581 drifts its train of empty mineral wagons on the downgrade past Forest Road playing field at Coalville Junction in 1962. Since that time only a single line of track remains, steam is no more and Bardon Hill, the county's highest point at 912 feet, has undergone some drastic surgery.

Photograph: Ron Hemsley

Nuneaton-based 49120, generally known as G2s by enginemen, was one of the former LNWR 0-8-0 class which regularly visited Coalville via Shackerstone junction.

Photograph: Ken Hunt

Displaced from main line duties by the advancing tide of diesel power it may have been, but Jubilee Class No. 45617 *Mauritius* was still an aristocrat among freight engines when she stayed overnight at Coalville in August 1964.

Photograph: Ron Hemsley

January 1962 and Coalville loco depot had a new arrival in the shape of 2F No. 58148, transferred from (3B) Bushbury after a visit to Derby Works, to work the Glenfield branch. Belying its great age in gleaming new paint, 58148 was to have a last moment of glory later that year when taking an enthusiasts' special through to West Bridge. Sadly, by December 1963 she was withdrawn from service, one of the last two of her class, and broken up by Cashmore's in September 1964.

Photograph: Ken Hunt

Neither by its looks nor performance could the 0-6-0 4F ever stir the senses. A Midland design of 1911, it was continued by the LMS until around 800 were working across the country. But shortcomings or no, the 4F was a real maid of all work - shunting, freight, local passenger or holiday specials, even substituting for a failed express locomotive was not unknown. On September 22nd, 1956, a Burton-on-Trent member of the class, No. 44528, bowls through Coalville on one of its regular runs, a fitted freight, bearing refreshment from local breweries to quench a few thirsts in the London area.

Photograph: Ken Hunt

Although no stranger to the Coalville area, the Hughes-designed 2-6-0 Class 5F were usually seen on fast freight work from Burton or on an occasional foray from Nuneaton along the Shackerstone branches. Making a welcome change from the regular passenger motive power, No. 42826, a Burton engine, was pictured in 1955 heading home down the bank from Bardon Hill station.

Photograph: Ken Hunt

Built around 1933, the 4-6-0 Patriot class were still hard at work on express duties 20 years on, mainly on the West Coast route and lines of the former London and North Western Railway. An occasional sighting of these locomotives was made on the Leicester to Burton line, No. 45539 *E. C. Trench* among them on a rather more prosaic working than when caught by the camera in July 1959 hurrying south after leaving Stafford.

Photograph: Ken Hunt

When someone had the idea of reducing the cab height of British Rail Standard locomotives the 19th Century, Midland Railway veterans were pensioned off at last. No. 78028, seen in Coalville shed yard in March 1964, and No. 78013 were of a 2-6-0 class built at Derby from 1953. The newcomers had little time to show their abilities. Nine months later Coalville shed closed to steam. The two engines continued to serve the West Bridge branch from Leicester shed until that also closed in May 1966.

Photograph: Ken Hunt

Another of Coalville's former Midland Railway 0-6-0s, No. 58163 was a long established resident on the local railscene, having been at Coalville from the early 1940s and at Burton (17B) for most of the 1930s. In this photograph of around 1953, the loco and her crew were emerging from the shed road for a morning's work shunting at Snibston and Whitwick collieries' sidings. Withdrawn in July 1961, 58163 was broken up at Derby Works in October 1962.

Photograph: Ken Hunt

Off to the sea. A day trip to Hunstanton passes Sinope headed by 44774, one of Stanier's numerous Black 5 4-6-0s. First introduced by the LMS in 1934, no fewer than 11 variations were subsequently produced as part of a class of 842 locomotives. Brooks's nurseries at Sinope can be seen to the left of the picture.

Photograph: Ron Hemsley

A rail enthusiasts special train visits Swannington station in the Spring of 1957, by which time the station buildings were derelict and the down waiting shelter a pile of rubble. Removal of platform edges revealed a number of stone blocks or sleepers used on the old Leicester and Swannington line more than a century before.

Photograph: Ken Hunt

Behind the elegant stone frontage of Ashby station its up platform was protected from the elements by an odd-looking, corrugated iron, five-bayed canopy. The reason for it was never forthcoming but when pictured in 1964, it had been in place for·at least 70 years.

Photogrpah: Barry Hilton

Ashby was connected by rail to Derby. From a junction on the Burton side of the station, this single line ran through Worthington, Tonge and Melbourne. Passenger services were withdrawn in 1930 but freight use continued for some years. By 1962, when this picture was taken looking towards the signal box, the Derby platform was fast disappearing beneath the undergrowth.

Photograph: Barry Hilton

Changes had been made at Gresley station shortly before this photo was taken in September 1956. Low footboards on carriages had disappeared so, for passenger safety, higher platforms made from old sleepers were added and a fence erected on the original platforms. This view is towards Leicester.

Photogrpah: H.C. Casserley

Shuttered and forlorn, the days of the former London North Western Railway station at Coalville East on the Charnwood Forest line were numbered. Still a reminder of times past when seen in June 1965, nothing now remains and modern homes now occupy the site as an extension of Oxford Street and Charwood Street.

Photograph: R. M. Casserley

On the return leg of the daily pick-up goods to Loughborough Derby Road, the Midland-built Class 2 No. 58247 takes a breather at Coalville East station and attracts an audience of youngsters from nearby Cambridge Street and Oxford Street on March 25th, 1950. Shortly, the loco would unhook from its train to fetch wagons of stone from Whitwick Quarry waiting in a siding behind the grassy bank on the right before continuing its journey towards Hugglescote junction.

Photograph: Ken Hunt

The fascination of steam attracted a countrywide following in the 1950s, enthusiasts interested in every aspect of the vast railway system travelling long distances to visit branches not usually accessible to the public. One such visit was that by the Rail Enthusiasts Club to Leicestershire in 1957 when their Charnwood Forester special was seen passing Coalville East station en route to Shepshed.

Photograph: Ken Hunt

Nature was taking over in June 1965 to cover the scars left behind by man. A station which once proudly advertised connections to Euston, Shepshed, lost its rail connection in 1963.

Photogrpah: R.M. Casserley

The slumbers of Shepshed station were disturbed when Leicester Railway Society took their special train along the Charnwood Forest line. Two years later, in 1963, the line was finally abandoned and the station area became an industrial site.

Photograph: Barry Hilton

Empty wagons are first shunted into a siding before No. 44148 (17C) can place a loaded van inside the goods shed at Coalville East while Mr. Issac Ward, station signalman from 1947 to closure in 1963, stands by the points. For some time in the 1950s the goods shed was a distribution point for Lyons Tea, a new office being added to the building. The scene has vanished completely. Whitwick Colliery spoil heap (extreme left), the footbridge in the background, the buildings and the original LNWR signals are all no more and a housing development now occupies the site.

Photograph: Ken Hunt

New houses in the New Parks area of Leicester contrast with the gallant old workhorse No. 58247 and the even older Glenfield tunnel in the summer of 1956. From its opening in 1832 the mile-long bore caused problems - the tall chimney of the loco on the inaugural train striking the roof, sending soot and cinders over distinguished passengers travelling in open wagons.

Photograph: Ken Hunt

MLS and SLS members organised a Leicestershire Rail Tour from Manchester Piccadilly in September 1962. To negotiate Glenfield tunnel it meant them boarding a train of 13 brakevans on their visit to the former Leicester and Swannington Railway terminus at West Bridge, Leicester. Bearing the Special's headboard, Coalville's No. 58148 had been specially polished up for the occasion.

Photogrpah: Horace Gamble

The signalman at Shackerstone Junction leans out to take the single-line staff from footplatemen as Stanier 8F No. 48386 heads south with coal from the Measham area. Joined here by the single line through Heather which gave connections to Coalville and Loughborough (seen bearing to the right behind the locomotive), the Ashby and Nuneaton Joint Railway made connection with former LNWR main line at Nuneaton.

Photograph: Ken Hunt

Shackerstone was the only station on the Ashby and Nuneaton Joint Line to boast a footbridge, and one solidly built in brick too. Accommodating a public right of way through the south Leicestershire countryside, the bridge and station are still very much in use today even though other features of this 1957 scene are no more.

Photograph: Ken Hunt

Diminutive it may have been, but No. 41516, an 0-4-0 saddletank design by Johnson for the Midland Railway, gave yeoman service in the Burton-on-Trent area on the tight curves which abounded in the sidings there. No. 1516, as she was in LMS days, even showed up on Coalville shed once. A marathon trip for such a gallant old-timer.

Photograph: H. C. Casserley

In the Leicester bay of the Burton-on-Trent station Stanier 2-6-2T Class 4MT 40207 awaits the off before taking its train across North West Leicestershire on a June day in 1953.

Photograph: H. C. Casserley

Cadley Hill Colliery near Castle Gresley, was one of the country's last strongholds of steam when this photograph was taken in September 1977. The view of pithead buildings and extensive sidings is lost under a cloud of exhaust from the locmotive, a Hunslet 0-6-0 saddletank (Works number 3851 of 1962), in what was then an everyday commonplace scene. Happily, the locomotive is still to be seen, though not in steam - in the exhibition hall at Snibston Discovery Park, Coalville.

Photograph: Kevin Lane

In addition to the many thousands of steam locomotives operated by the Big Four (LMS, LNER, GWR, SR) and British Rail which succeeded them, there were others which rarely earned a mention - the Industrials. Smaller, rugged engines often with a saddletank to carry water, they worked away often unseen in difficult situations throughout the country - in gas works, engineering sites, ironstone and quarry workings, power stations and coal mines. Privately owned they worked their internal networks and took out to the main line the loaded wagons. Ellistown Colliery's *Wellington* was a typical example, built by Andrew Barclay in 1940 and still hard at work in 1965.

Photograph: Horace Gamble

Roadstone from Bardon Quarry is still as much in demand today as it was in October 1977 when this Robert Stephenson and Hawthorne-built 0-6-0 diesel hydraulic was pictured at the A50 road crossing. Barely visible in the background lies one of the quarry's old steam locos while to the right homes in the former Old Row can be glimpsed.

Photograph: Kevin Lane

Snibston Colliery, Coalville, and another load of coal moves out from under the screens bound for the exchange sidings on the main line behind a Hunslet 0-6-0 diesel loco in 1977. The rear of the Midland Red bus garage is to the right of the photograph.

Photograph: Kevin Lane

Bagworth signal box stands guard over the rubble of the demolished Bagworth and Ellistown station platforms either side of the two lines in the foreground. Beyond, the headstocks of Bagworth Colliery loom large on the horizon as a Rolls Royce 0-6-0 diesel loco pulls out a string of loaded wagons bound for power stations in the Birmingham area on a March day in 1978. Around a decade later the colliery was closed down. The last coal mine in Leicestershire.

Photograph: Kevin Lane

An eerie silence fell on Coalville's locomotive shed when its last steam locomotives departed in September 1964. For a few months more the building was used as an occasional stabling point for diesel locos such as D5255 and D7537 pictured in July 1965 before demolition in October that same year. Any indications of the site's long association with steam railways has long since been wiped out and an industrial complex stands there today.

Photograph: Ken Hunt

Before the advent of paper or card tickets, passengers on the Leicester and Swannington Railway were issued with octagonal brass tokens in return for payment of fares . (actual size - 35mm across)

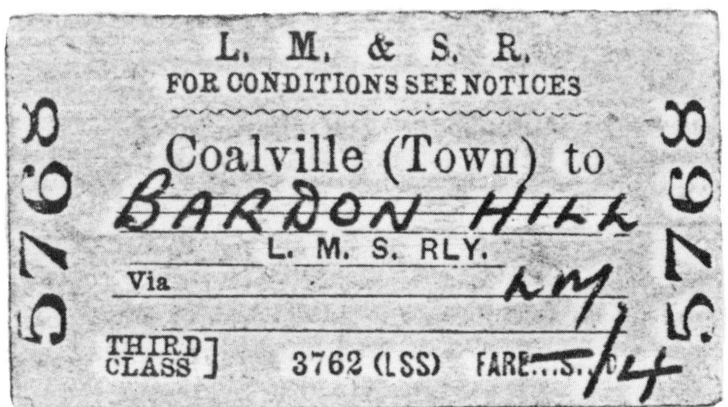

Bardon Hill was the first station on the Leicester - Burton line to be closed and this was the last ticket issued from Coalville. It is signed on the reverse by station clerk, John Lycett.

Railway Talk

The following are extracts from taped reminiscences collected by The Leicester Oral History Archive during the 1980s. The railwaymen concerned worked for various companies operating in, around and out of the Leicestershire area.

My father started on the railway in 1877 at the age of about 17 or 18. His first job, after cleaning, was firing on the Manchester expresses. It wasn't long before they got on the footplate in those days. The engines were primitive with very little cab and he would tell me that when the old time drivers put their heads out the side of the cab, their long beards blew back in the wind and they had to hold down the bowler hats they wore.

The first old driver he worked with told him to fetch himself a length of rope. When he asked why, he was told it was to tie himself on as there was a danger of being thrown off at speed. The cabs were pretty well open with just a bit of weather-board at the front. They called the engines Hellfire Jacks and they were a bit rough with a big, single, eight foot wheel which meant that they used to roll about quite a lot.

If you go back to 1916, before I started on the railway, we had a very severe blizzard which came on a Sunday night, March 28th. It filled all the roads up and knocked all the telegraph poles down. It filled the cuttings up on the Bourne line and that line was closed for a fortnight. In the winter of 1946/47, I remember getting down from the engine and being up to the armpits in snow. When I was at Witham, somebody had left the drain cover off a cesspit and this feller got off the engine into snow and he dropped down the drain up to his waist.

When I was about 16 we went on a five shilling trip to Leeds to see my father's sister. On the return journey, as the engine had a very heavy train on, it stalled on a steep incline between Doncaster and Sheffield, I think it was. Every time the driver opened the regulator and took the brake off, the engine rolled back. This went on for about half an hour. Eventually Dad got out and walked up the track to the footplate - he knew the crew. After about five or ten minutes, we started moving. I wondered what Driver Webb had done to get the train away but he never did tell me. All he said was: Well, when I got on, the old girl knew me and thought, here comes old Jack! How he got it going I shall never know.

On the old Glenfield line there were four trains a day to and from Desford and Leicester:- 8.25 to Leicester, 1.30 to Desford, 2.08 from Desford and the last train was 5.30 from Leicester which brought the factory girls home. It was dark in the Glenfield tunnel at any time of the day or year but the rule was that the last train must have its carriages lit up every time it went through the tunnel. The lamps hung from the ceiling and someone had to get to the top of the coaches to light them. They were just wicks floating in oil. I was only a kid at the time but always wondered why it was that only the last train had to be lit. It was supposed to be something to do with regulations drawn up when the line started in the 1830s and it had been followed ever since.

I remember one day down at Desford station, some of the lads and some older men were kicking a football about at dinner time. The passenger train from Burton to Leicester came into the station. It had got a Class 2 engine on it which had a very long chimney. While it stood in the station a lad kicked the ball and it dropped down the chimney. When the driver opened the throttle, whoosh! out shot the ball!

When I started on the railway, it was a job for life. When you tried to get a job you had to have three character references before they would accept you. One from the school master, one from the scout master, another from a clergyman or someone like that. Then you went to Derby to be scrutinised. After the interview, the only indication that you'd got the job was that they'd say: Now, young man, I want you to go over that bridge and go through the door marked Clothing Department. That was the only indication. When you got home your mother would ask: Did you go over the bridge? They didn't say whether you'd got the job they just told you to go over the bridge. Of course, there was written confirmation later.

I started on the Monday morning and was called into the office and told that I was a lucky chap because he wanted the vacancies for his drivers' sons. In those days if your dad had a good job on the railways you stood a good chance of going engine cleaning, for a start. I was engine cleaning for years. I started in 1927 for thirty-six shillings a week. We didn't get a rise until we were twenty and then it went up by a shilling a day until it reached forty-two shillings. You then stayed on forty-two shillings until you'd done three hundred and thirteen firing turns. Then you got half-a-crown extra which made it nine and six a day. We had to pass exams to become firemen and drivers. The rules and regulations were the hardest things to learn. There were so many of them. As soon as anything went wrong anywhere, a new rule came out.

There were very complicated regulations which governed signalling procedures, much the same as they are today. A driver only took an exam once but a signalman was examined in the rules and regulations every year. If he didn't pass he'd be taken off the job. They might have found him another job as a porter or something, if they had one, but until he passed that exam he couldn't go back to being a signalman.

In 1946 I was passed for driving. I was thirty-seven. Promotion was very slow especially before the war. It would be about twenty-four years before you went driving regularly. The wages altered as time went on. To get the top money for firing, which was twelve shillings a day (that was also the minimum rate for driving) you had to do three hundred and thirteen trips to get nine shillings and sixpence, another three hundred and thirteen for ten and six, six hundred and twenty-six for eleven shillings and maybe four or five years for twelve shillings a day. It took nine or ten years to get the top rate for firing. I never did reach my top rate because during the first year firing, I only get ten or twelve trips. As chaps retired you might get a few more trips. It could take a long while to get all the required trips in before you became a driver. The top rate for driver, before the war, was four pounds ten shillings a week.

In about 1932 the railways were in difficulties so they asked the staff to take a percentage drop in wages. We agreed to have a drop of sixpence in the pound. They promised to pay us back when things got better. I'm still waiting for mine after more than sixty years!

The railways used to own hundreds of horses. Deliveries were made by horse and cart right up until the middle of the 1950s. They were beautiful, big shire horses and were also sometimes used for shunting. If a wagon in a goods yard needed moving from one side to the other and there was a railway horse there, you'd put a chain on him and hook him on to the wagon. A horse could pull a ten ton wagon to position it onto a different siding. The horses were better looked after than the men. They had proper stables, they were well fed and each horse had a staff number stamped on a hoof. There were record books which contained the pet name of the horse, its date of birth, its description, all the various vaccinations, any illness and they were examined weekly by the vet. Those horses had ten days' holiday a year and when I first started on the railway we only got one week.

Another creature that worked for the railway was the cat. There was an official station cat at any depot which had a grain store. They were allowed, according to how much floor space there was, one, two or three cats. Each cat was allowed one pint of milk per week to be paid for out of petty cash. There was no money allowed for food as the cats were expected to make their own arrangements for that. They were official cats and on the books. We had a lady station cat once who had a boyfriend over the road and she had kittens quite frequently. Sometimes members of staff would take a kitten or there would be a request from another station. We would get a call saying: Have you got any kittens? Our cat's been run over by a train. If we had, we would send one off in a box to become their station cat.

One of the regular jobs in the old days was farm removals. When a farmer moved, especially if he was buying another farm, it was not just him, his wife, the children and the car. There was the tractor, the plough, the livestock, foodstuff, the implements etc. This used to be a wonderful operation to do. I have been a signalman and seen a farm train go by. It was fascinating. There was the locomotive, immediately behind would be a passenger coach holding the farmer's family and the dog - to a farmer the dog isn't an animal, he's a member of the management. Behind the passenger coach there would be perhaps three or four cattle trucks with the cows and sheep and a couple of horses in a horse box. Behind them would be the goods wagons with the tractor, the tools and various machinery. So you'd got a nice mixed train to move the whole farm. It wouldn't come cheap because any special operation naturally costs more than a normal one but farm removals were quite common.

What always used to be an event was the circus trains. They always had special trains. One night they loaded the elephants but when the elephant van arrived at Loughborough, it was what we called a flat. There wasn't a thing standing on it except for the three elephants chained to the heavy bolsters across the wagon. On the journey the elephants had torn down the van and thrown the pieces away.

We used to cook breakfast on a shovel, a regular thing for years. You could do it while you were moving, coasting down a big incline but it was a bit risky as you could lose your pan. We would have bacon and egg and sausage. When I pulled up at St Pancras passengers used to smell it when they were coming by me. They'd come off the coaches and say: Oh boy, I bet that was great. And it was!

Breakfast cooked on a shovel tastes lovely, especially on a crisp, frosty morning round about October time. We'd perhaps get booked on about five in the morning and when we got to Whetstone or Ashby or somewhere like that, we'd cook our breakfast. You'd a have a frizzling tin and put that on the shovel.

When I was down the Great Northern once, I'd got eggs and a lovely, big slice of gammon for my breakfast. We used go through to Bottesford before we had a chance to cook and that wouldn't be before eleven o'clock. We got into a siding and I was ready for my breakfast. I put it on the shovel, put it in the fire box and it all slid right off so I lost the lot. We very rarely cooked while we were on the move.

Before the war and for some time after there were a lot of counterfeit coins about. By the booking office window was a stiff piece of brass bolted to the counter and you could test a coin by putting it in a slot and trying to bend it. Anyone used to handling coins could recognise forgeries straight away. In the old days it was a common thing to find sixpences being counterfeited. I remember a man coming up to the window and putting a half crown down. I said to him: That's a dud, mate. I asked him should I test it for him and he said not to and put it away and found me another. It was either that or he didn't get a ticket.

Leicester was a top hat station. When the station master was in his office, he'd have his striped trousers on and a black jacket. When he needed to go out to meet a posh train or a posh person, he would put on his tail coat and top hat. If he left the station to go to lunch or for some other reason, he would wear his bowler hat so he wouldn't look too conspicuous.

I worked at a little station and every Friday morning a box of fish arrived destined for the nearby monastery. It was my job, as a lad, to load this fish onto a barrow and deliver it. I had to wait while they opened the box because they always gave me a piece of fish for myself, and a blessing - that made me feel good. The first few times when I took the fish home, I had to explain to my mother that I had come by it honestly and not pinched it.

We were eating fish in Loughborough at six o'clock which had been landed at Hull or Grimsby that same morning. We had six special trains of fish every night apart from the one in the day-time. The day-time train arrived at 4.06 and had to leave at 4.11 so we had five minutes to unload all Loughborough's fish. Then I had to have it entered up. I went for my tea-break at 4.15, so it was all done pretty smartish, believe me. I didn't want to miss my tea!

We had train loads of coal which was kept at the loco sheds. I guess that a place like Leicester would have between eighty and a hundred wagons of coal a week with ten tons in each. When a locomotive needed coaling it used to go under a stage and the coal was tipped down a chute into the tender. There was a fairly rapid turn round.

Before nationalisation each company's locomotives were designed to burn the coal from the local coalfield. Towards the end of the steam era, when locos were used all over the country, one trouble was that they weren't steaming properly because they'd got the wrong sort of coal.

Some firemen are better than others. A good fireman would always have plenty of steam, know where he was and look out for signals etc. A poor fireman wouldn't have a clue. There were only one or two poor ones that I remember who I don't think would ever had made drivers.

It would take about four or five tons of coal to get to London and back from Leicester. You'd have about eight tubs containing perhaps half a ton of coal each. When we had good coal, before and during the war, it averaged at about 39lbs of coal per mile on Atlantics on the Great Central. With bad coal you'd get a dirty fire and the engine wouldn't steam. The Pacifics on the Great Northern used to average about 34lbs to the mile or so one of my mates told me.

I've driven all sorts. I only drove Pacifics once or twice but I've driven Atlantics, Green Arrows and the Footballers which started at Leicester. 2848 was the one, then 2849. The early ones were called Grimsby Town, Sheffield United, Derby County, Darlington - I don't remember them all. There was a brass football on the side of the engine with the name over it.

Driving a steam engine was always a dirty job and could be cold in winter. The fireman was kept warm by the fire but not the driver. When you were coming back from London and the coal was low behind you, cold air would whip through and you'd get it on your back as well as getting no heat from the fire. On one particular engine - an eight coupled wheel the engine was - on the left hand side where the driver sat, there was a steel column housing the brake or some other thing and that also shielded the fire from the driver and he would be perished.

The relationship between railwaymen is like being members of the same club. A lot of railwaymen, especially on the operational side, would often say: I'm getting paid to pursue my hobby. There are a lot people of all ages, today, who willingly pay to drive a steam engine, don't they?

Thanks go to Mantle Community Arts for access to the above memories.

The publishers are grateful to the following who subscribed to this book in advance. We would also like to thank those who have been waiting for some time, for their patience .

Jennifer Adcock, Coalville, Leics.
Mrs D Allen, Coalville, Leics.
Mrs P Allett, Bagworth, Leics.
Mr N Allsopp, Uttoxeter, Staffs.
Mrs S Atton, Wigston, Leics.
Malcolm J Bailiss, Hugglescote, Leics.
Pete Baker, Hugglescote, Leics.
Mr George Barkby.
Mr C Barnes, Leicester.
Mr R J Barry, Oadby, Leics.
Miss P Bates, Sileby, Leics.
Mrs A Baxter, Ibstock, Leics.
P Bosworth, Kegworth, Leics.
Mr G Bradford, Whitwick, Leics.
M J Bradford, Ravenstone, Leics.
Mrs P Bramley, Glenfield, Leics.
J M Branson, Wigston, Leics.
Mr C R D Broome, Leicester.
Mr R A Broome, Leicester.
Mr J Brooks, Coalville, Leics.
Adrian Broster, Coalville, Leics.
Mr D A Brown, Ashby de la Zouch, Leics.
Mr P G Browne, Ellistown, Leics.
R I Cassie, Leicester.
R Camp, Narborough, Leics.
Mr J Chambers, Harston, Cambridge.
Roger Chapman, Kimcote, Leics.
Roy T Chapman, Uttoxeter, Staffs.
Mr W Chell, Birstall, Leics.
Mr D Colley, Whitwick, Leics.
Dave Collins, Leicester.
Mr Robert Crow, Oadby, Leics.
Ian Davie, Shepshed, Leics.
Mr G A Dawson, Broughton Astley, Leics.
Chris Deacon, Leics.
Mrs D M Deane, Donington le Heath, Leics.
Mr M Dickman, Leicester.
Mr R W Dixey, Countesthorpe, Leics.
Mr L L Edwards, Coalville, Leics.
John Elliot, Coalville, Leics.
Mr Joe Ennis, Gillingham, Kent.
R Ensor, Donisthorpe, Leics.
D C Everett, Shepshed, Leics.
Sue E Finney, Coalville, Leics.
Mr J Fisher, Burton on Trent, Staffs.
Mr E Fowler, Sileby, Leics.
Malcolm Fox, Leicester Forest East.
Mr J Freer, Earl Shilton, Leics.
M D French, Fleckney, Leics.
R Gamble, Coalville, Leics.

Mr P Geary, Sutton Bonnington, Leics.
Mrs M Gee, Castle Donington, Leics.
John K Gibbins, Coalville, Leics.
Mr M Gill, Whitwick, Leics.
Mrs J P Gillespie, Leicester.
Trevor Goodman, Leicester.
Derek J Grant, Nottingham.
Mr K A Gray, Carlton Miniott, N Yorks.
Mr J A Griffiths, Leicester Forest East.
Barrie Hall, Ashby de la Zouch, Leics.
Mrs M Hamson, Burbage, Leics.
Mr A T Hannant, Coalville, Leics.
Mr A J Harrison, Hugglescote, Leics.
Rev E J Hart, Thringstone, Leics.
E Harwood-Kellaway, Sharnford, Leics.
Mark Higginson, West Hallam, Derby.
Pam Holmes, Coalville, Leics.
Mr B Horwood, Burnham, Bucks
A W Ingram, Wigston, Leics.
C R Insley, Leics.
Roger Insley, Leics.
Barry Kendall, Cosby, Leics.
Mr B A Kibble, Glenfield, Leics.
Mr G Knight, Ashby de la Zouch, Leics.
Mr & Mrs C S Lambert, Loughborough, Leics.
Mrs P Lambourne, Cropston, Leics.
G J Lancaster, Coventry.
Mr H Leck, Coalville, Leics.
S Lee, Loughborough, Leics.
J Legrys, Leics.
Mr B E Leo, Oadby, Leics.
Ian Lowe, Loughborough, Leics.
Mr A M Lindsey, Enderby, Leics.
Roger Lloyd, Wolverhampton.
Mr P A Lord, Glenfield, Leics.
Andy Lowe, Loughborough, Leics.
Mr R Martin, Groby, Leics.
Chris Matchett, Whitwick, Leics.
Rev B Matthews, Thringstone, Leics.
Mr B Miller, Swadlincote, Derbys.
Mrs D Milloy, Leicester.
Barry A Morley, Leicester.
A Moore, Narborough, Leics.
L M Murray, Loughborough, Leics.
Mr John M Neal, Hathern, Leics.
Tony Norwell, Coalville, Leics.
Professor P R Odell, Ipswich.
Mr & Mrs R E S Ottey, Glenfield, Leics.
Mrs Ann Parks, Anstey, Leics.
Vivien Parry, Ashby de la Zouch, Leics.
Mr Bob Payne, Melton Mowbray, Leics.
Steve Peace, Hugglescote, Leics.
Mr E S Pearce, Coalville, Leics.
Terry Pearce, Whetstone, Leics.
Mr J R Pearson, Coalville, Leics.
Mr L V Phillips, Ibstock, Leics.
Mrs D H Pilkington, Leicester.
Mr B Pilmore, Chaddesden, Derbys

Mr E G Pink, Coalville, Leics.
Miss R J Plaskett, Leicester.
Michael Platts, Whitwick, Leics.
R J Pollock, Ashby de la Zouch, Leics.
Andrew Poole, Loughborough, Leics.
Mark Postins, Ibstock, Leics.
K G Prior, Marlow, Bucks.
D L Quarterman, Ravenstone, Leics.
Mrs S A Quincey, Leicester.
Mrs B Randon, Ashby de la Zouch, Leics.
Mr John Reed, Donington le Heath, Leics.
Mrs A Rice, Chellaston, Derbys.
G R Rice, Ashby de la Zouch, Leics.
Rev J & Mrs C Richardson, Hugglescote, Leics.
Mr M G Richardson, Leicester.
In memory of James Robinson, Hugglescote, Leics.
Martin Sargent, Snarestone, Leics.
Mr E Sharpe, Leicester.
G Sherratt, Moira, Leics.
Sid Sherriff, Leicester.
Mrs D Shilcock, Glenfield, Leics.
P R Simmonds, Shepshed, Leics.
Mr P A Slater, Bude, Cornwall.
Mr D A Smith, Glenfield, Leics.
Mrs H S Smith, Drayton, Norfolk.
J Smith, Ravenstone, Leics.
Mrs J M Smith, Leicester.
Mr K H Smith, Coalville, Leics.
Peter Smith, Coalville, Leics.
Mr P G Smith, Coalville, Leics.
Mr P W Smith, Colchester, Essex.
Mr & Mrs R K Smith, Nuneaton, Warks.
C Southwood, Hugglescote, Leics.
E J Spencer, Barrow on Soar, Leics.
R W Staines, Kirkby Mallory, Leics.
Desmond Starbuck, Coalville, Leics.
J R Steven, Whitwick, Leics.
Mr D R Stocker, Wigston Fields, Leics.
Mr P Stoddart, Leicester.
Phil Tatham, Ashby de la Zouch, Leics.
Mr Leopold Taylor, Swadlincote, Derbys.
Geoff Tovell, Hugglescote, Leics.
Peter Tovell, Bolton, Lancs.
Mr P Tranmer, Whetstone, Leics.
Mr K S Tyers, Oakham, Rutland.
Mr J Verrier, Glenfield, Leics.
Martin Wain, Rothley, Leics.
Joseph Walker.
Mr Shane Wheatley.
Mr & Mrs F Whiting, Grantham, Lincs
Mr R Widdowson, Exton, Devon.
N J Wilkins, Long Whatton, Leics.
Brian Williams, Ellistown, Leics.
Mr S Woodcock, Leicester.
Mrs A E Woolerton, Market Bosworth, Leics.
Mr & Mrs Wortley, Coalville, Leics.
Mrs Ena Young, Market Harborough, Leics.
C J York, Woodhouse Eaves, Leics.